Relax with
Classical Piano

33 Beautiful Pieces

Selected by
Samantha Ward

ED 13850
ISMN 979-0-2201-3682-5
ISBN 978-1-84761-398-1

www.schott-music.com

Mainz · London · Berlin · Madrid · New York · Paris · Prague · Tokyo · Toronto
© 2016 SCHOTT MUSIC Ltd, London · Printed in Germany

ED 13850
British Library Cataloguing-in-Publication Data.
A catalogue record for this book is available from the British Library
ISMN 979-0-2201-3682-5
ISBN 978-1-84761-398-1
© 2016 Schott Music Ltd, London

Cover design by www.josellopis.com
French translation: Michaëla Rubi
German translation: Heike Brühl
Printed in Germany S&Co.9285

Contents

Introduction

Schott Music's *Relax With* series is designed to help you unwind with some of the piano repertoire's greatest works, alongside lesser known pieces from the Baroque period right through to the 20th century. I have tried to include as many different styles and techniques as possible, whilst remaining within the boundaries of 'relaxing' pieces of music. It has been particularly enjoyable for me to delve into new works in producing these five collections, and to be able to include pieces by the most famous composers as well as by those who are less well known, such as Johanna Senfter, Xaver Scharwenka and, in the Folk collection, works from around the world by Georges Ivanovitch Gurdjieff and Thomas de Hartmann. I hope you enjoy the collections and that you too get to know new pieces along the way.

In this anthology, I explore relaxing classical works and I have decided to introduce you to a number of transcriptions of wonderful pieces originally written for other instruments, such as Mozart's clarinet concerto and the beautiful *Lacrimosa* from Mozart's Requiem.

Samantha Ward

Samantha Ward is a British Concert pianist, and founder and Artistic Director of the international festival and summer school, *Piano Week*. For more information, please visit **www.samanthaward.org**

Introduction

La collection « Moments détente » des éditions Schott est conçue pour vous aider à vous relaxer grâce à quelques-unes des plus grandes œuvres du répertoire pour piano ainsi que d'autres moins connues, de la période baroque à nos jours. Je me suis attaché à inclure dans cette sélection des techniques et des styles aussi variés que possible sans perdre de vue les propriétés « relaxantes » de la musique. J'ai eu beaucoup de plaisir à rechercher de nouveaux morceaux dans la perspective des cinq recueils de cette collection et me suis réjoui d'avoir la possibilité de choisir aussi bien des œuvres des compositeurs les plus célèbres que celles d'autres bien moins connus tels que Johanna Senfter ou Xaver Scharwenka ou, parmi les musiques du monde, celles de Georges Ivanovitch Gurdjieff et Thomas de Hartmann. J'espère que vous apprécierez ces recueils et qu'ils vous permettront à vous aussi de découvrir de nouvelles œuvres.

Dans cette anthologie, je propose des œuvres classiques aux propriétés relaxantes parmi lesquelles un certain nombre de pièces merveilleuses initialement écrites pour d'autres instruments, en particulier le concerto pour clarinette de Mozart et le magnifique *Lacrimosa* de son *Requiem*.

Samantha Ward

Fondatrice et directrice artistique du festival international et des cours d'été « Piano Week », Samantha Ward est une pianiste concertiste britannique. Vous trouverez davantage d'informations sur son site **www.samanthaward.org**

Einleitung

Mit der Reihe *Relax With* von Schott Music kann man mit vielen bekannten Klavierwerke sowie einigen weniger bekannten Stücken vom Barock bis zum 20. Jahrhundert entspannen. Ich habe versucht, so viele verschiedene Stilrichtungen und Techniken wie möglich zu berücksichtigen und dabei trotzdem den Aspekt der Entspannung nicht aus den Augen zu verlieren. Bei der Zusammenstellung der fünf Sammlungen war es für mich besonders schön, neue Werke kennen zu lernen und Stücke der ganz großen, aber auch Stücke von weniger bekannten Komponisten wie z. B. Johanna Senfter, Xaver Scharwenka und – in der Volksmusik-Sammlung – Werke aus aller Welt von Georges Ivanovitch Gurdjieff und Thomas de Hartmann in die Bände aufzunehmen. Ich wünsche Ihnen viel Spaß mit den Sammlungen und hoffe, dass auch Sie darin einige neue Stücke finden.

In dieser Anthologie sind entspannende klassische Werke enthalten sowie einige Bearbeitungen hervorragender Stücke, die ursprünglich für andere Instrumente geschrieben wurden, z. B. Mozarts Klarinettenkonzert und das *Lacrimosa* aus Mozarts Requiem.

Samantha Ward

Samantha Ward ist eine britische Konzertpianistin sowie die Gründerin und künstlerische Leiterin von *Piano Week*, einem internationalen Festival und Ferienkurs. Weitere Informationen finden Sie im Internet unter **www.samanthaward.org**

Andante Grazioso

Wolfgang Amadeus Mozart (1756–1791)
Arr.: Hans-Günther Heumann

From the Schott edition *The Classical Piano Method: Method Book 2* (ED 13382)

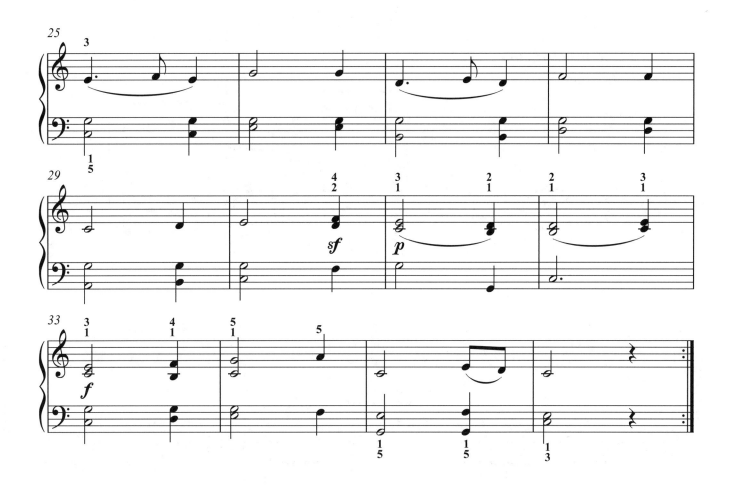

Air Russe

Un poco Adagio
(♩ = 60–66)

Johann Nepomuk Hummel
(1778–1837)

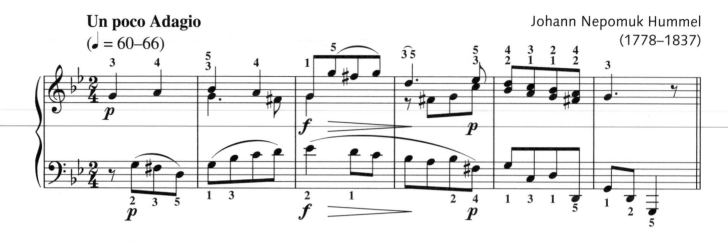

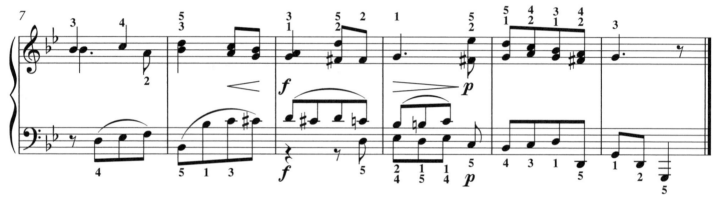

From the Schott edition *Classical Piano Anthology 1* (ED 13234)

Siciliano in G minor

August Eberhard Müller
(1767–1817)

From the Schott edition *Classical Piano Anthology 1* (ED 13234)

Adagio
KV 356

Wolfgang Amadeus Mozart
(1756–1791)

From the Schott edition *Classical Piano Anthology 3* (ED 13440)

This page is left blank to save an unnecessary page turn.

Symphony No. 7 "Unfinished"
2nd theme from the 1st movement

Franz Schubert
(1797–1828)
Arr.: Hans-Günther Heumann

Allegro moderato ♩ = 92

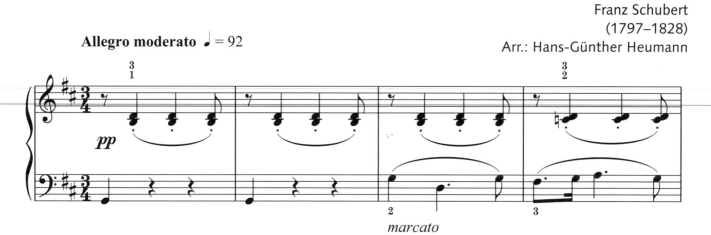

marcato

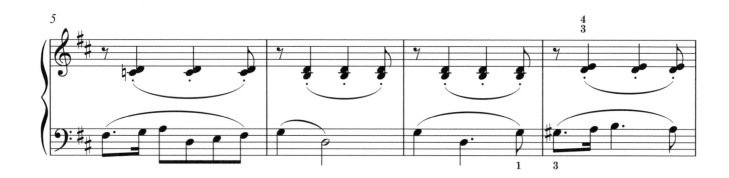

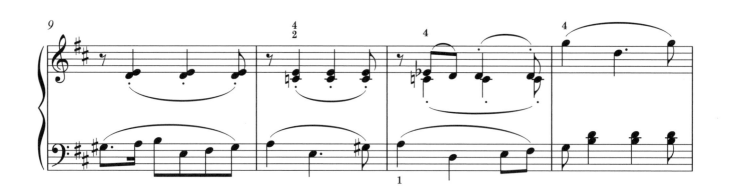

From the Schott edition *The Classical Piano Method: Repertoire Collection 3* (ED 13573)

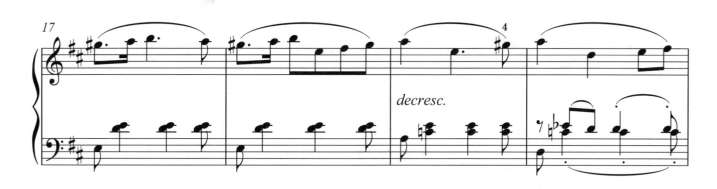

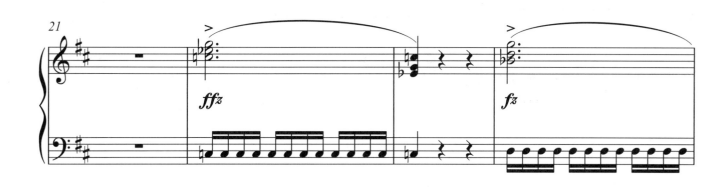

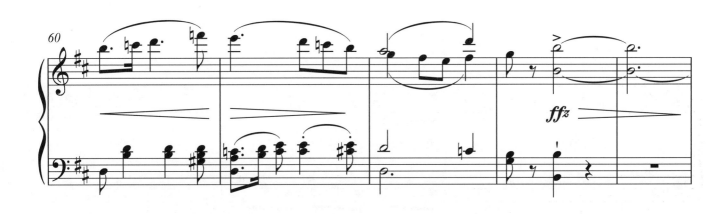

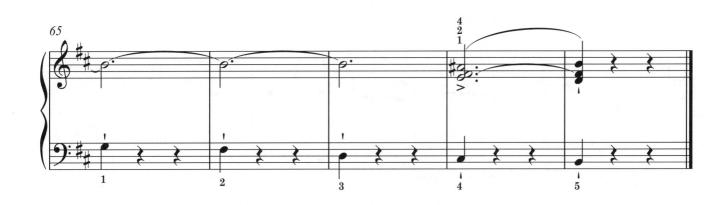

Andante

from *Sonatina* in C major

Muzio Clementi
(1752–1832)

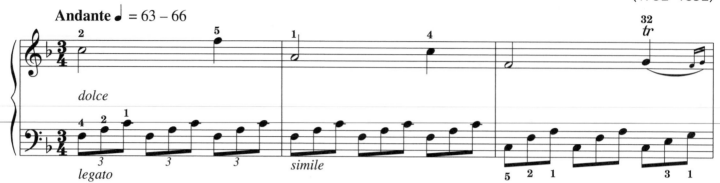

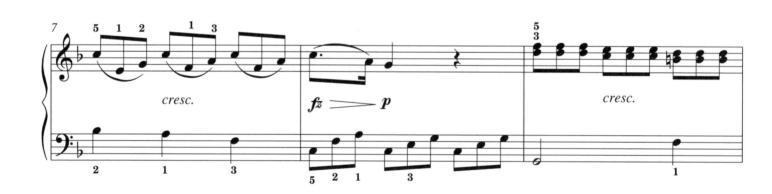

From the Schott edition *Best of Piano Classics* (ED 9060)

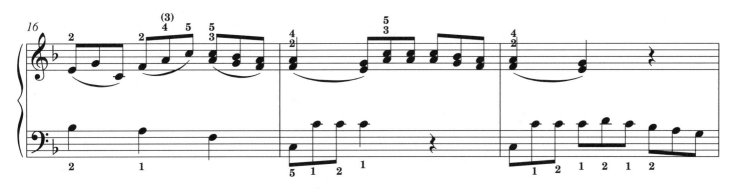

Menuet
G major

Ludwig van Beethoven
(1770–1827)

Men. D. C.

From the Schott edition 6 *Menuette* (ED0 277)

This page is left blank to save an unnecessary page turn.

Symphony No. 7

A major, theme from the 2nd movement
Op. 92

Allegretto ♩ = 60

Ludwig van Beethoven (1770–1827)
Arr.: Hans-Günther Heumann

From the Schott edition *The Classical Piano Method: Repertoire Collection 3* (ED 13573)

(2nd time
sempre dim.)

Lacrimosa
from *Requiem*
KV 626

Wolfgang Amadeus Mozart
(1756–1791)
Arr.: Hans-Günther Heumann

Andante moderato ♪ = 104

La - cri-mo - sa di - es il - la, qua re-sur - get ex fa-vil - la ju - di can - dus ho - mo re - us. La - cri-mo - sa di - es il - la, qua re-sur - get ex fa-vil - la ju - di-can - dus ho - mo re - us. Hu - ic er - go

From the Schott edition *Pianissimo: Eine kleine Nachtmusik* (ED 20764)

Gott erhalte
from the String Quartet in C major
Hob. III:77

Joseph Haydn
(1732–1809)
Arr.: Joseph Haydn

From the Schott edition *Pianissimo: Eine kleine Nachtmusik* (ED 20764)

Ständchen
„Leise flehen meine Lieder"
Serenade

Franz Schubert
(1797–1828)

Translation of German Lyrics:

My songs beckon softly / through the night to you; / below in the quiet grove, /Come to me, beloved!
The rustle of slender leaf tips whispers / in the moonlight; / Do not fear the evil spying /of the betrayer, my dear.
Do you hear the nightingales call? / Ah, they beckon to you, / With the sweet sound of their singing / they beckon to you for me.
They understand the heart's longing, / know the pain of love, / They calm each tender heart / with their silver tones.
Let them also stir within your breast, / beloved, hear me! / Trembling I wait for you, / Come, please me!

From the Schott edition *Schubert: Selected Works* (ED 510)

Waltz B minor
Op. 18/6

Franz Schubert
(1797–1828)

From the Schott edition *Best of Piano Classics* (ED 9060)

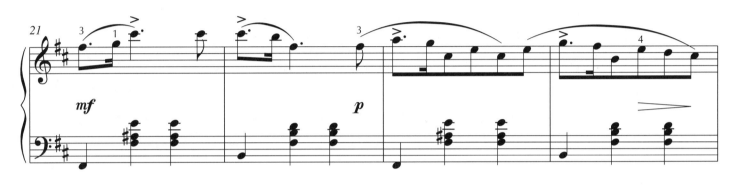

Adagio

Hob. XVII: 9

Joseph Haydn
(1732–1809)

From the Schott edition *Classical Piano Anthology 2* (ED 13436)

Easy Sonata
C major

Wolfgang Amadeus Mozart
(1756–1791)

From the Schott edition *Pianissimo: Für Elise* (ED 20044)

Concerto for Clarinet and Orchestra

A major, 2nd movement

KV 622

Wolfgang Amadeus Mozart
(1756–1791)
Arr.: Hans-Günter Heumann

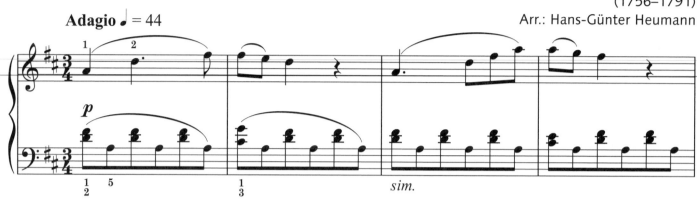

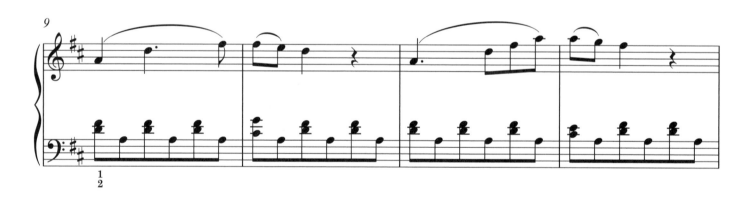

From the Schott edition *Pianissimo: Eine kleine Nachtmusik* (ED 20764)

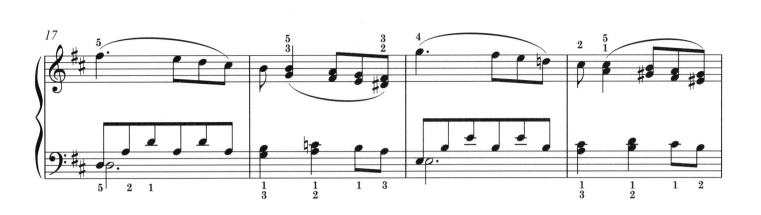

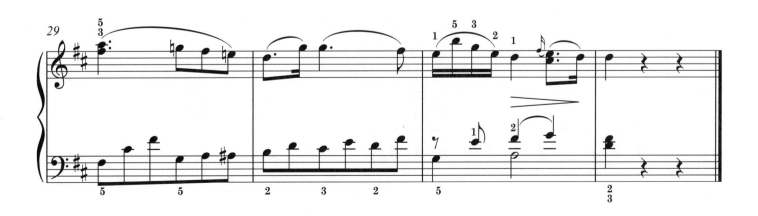

Concerto for Piano and Orchestra No. 21

C major, 2nd movement

KV 467

Wolfgang Amadeus Mozart
(1756–1791)
Arr.: Hans-Günter Heumann

From the Schott edition *Pianissimo: Eine kleine Nachtmusik* (ED 20764)

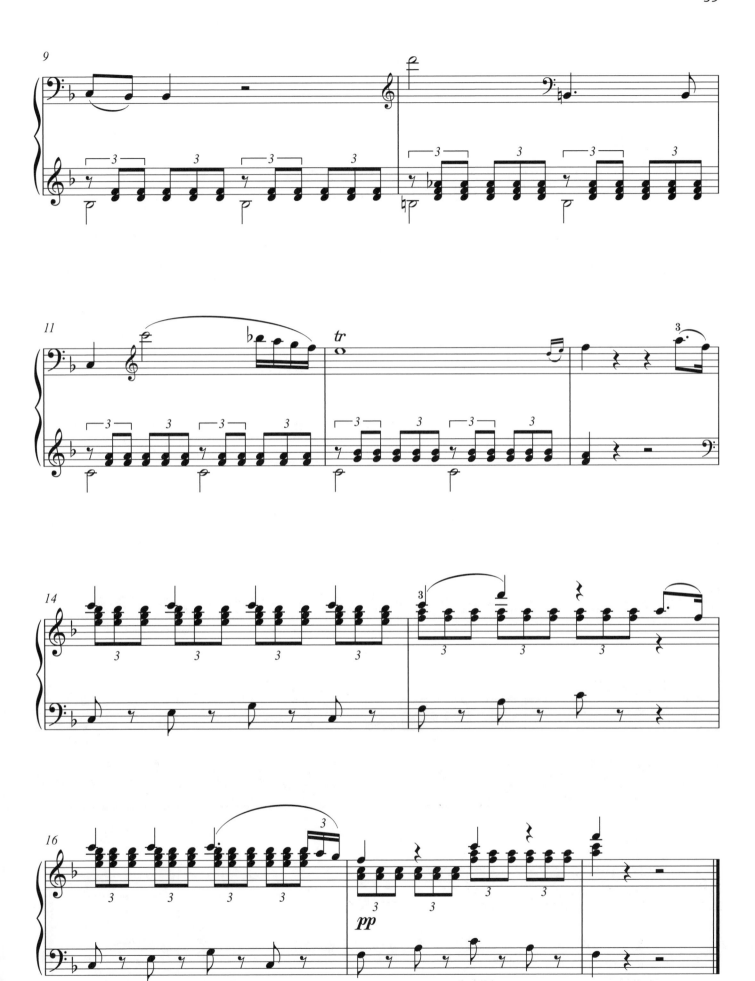

Menuet
Op. 13/5

Luigi Boccherini
(1743–1805)
Arr.: Hans-Günter Heumann

From the Schott edition *Pianissimo: Eine kleine Nachtmusik* (ED 20764)

Trio

D.C. al Fine

Andante
from Sonata in C major, KV 545

Wolfgang Amadeus Mozart
(1756–1791)

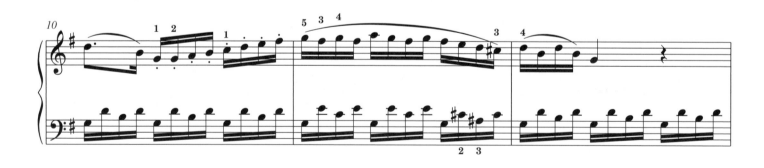

From the Schott edition *Best of Piano Classics* (ED 9060)

Bagatelle No. 5

from 6 *Bagatelles*, Op. 126

Ludwig van Beethoven
(1770–1827)

Quasi Allegretto

From the Schott edition *Six Bagatelles* (EDO 273)

This page is left blank to save an unnecessary page turn.

Concerto for Piano and Orchestra No. 5

E♭ major, 2nd movement

Op. 73

Ludwig van Beethoven
(1770–1827)
Arr.: Hans-Günter Heumann

From the Schott edition *Pianissimo: Eine kleine Nachtmusik* (ED 20764)

Bagatelle

G minor
Op. 119/1

Ludwig van Beethoven
(1770–1827)

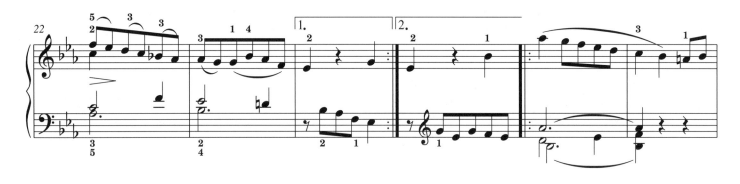

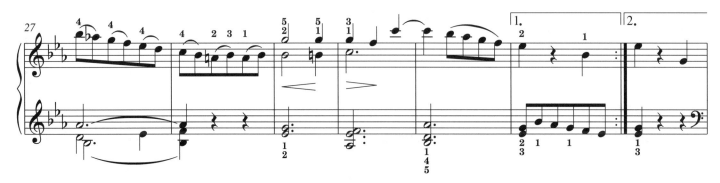

From the Schott edition *Best of Piano Classics* (ED 9060)

Für Elise
WoO 59

Ludwig van Beethoven
(1770–1827)

From the Schott edition *Best of Piano Classics* (ED 9060)

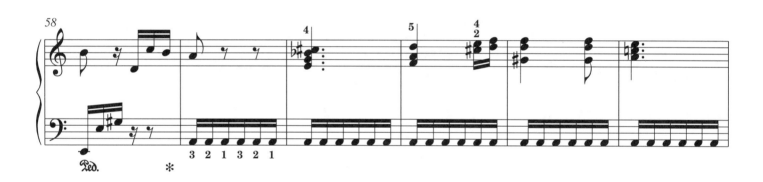

Bagatelle No. 3

from 6 *Bagatelles*, Op. 126

Ludwig van Beethoven
(1770–1827)

Andante
Cantabile e grazioso

From the Schott edition *Six Bagatelles* (EDO 273)

Adagio
from Sonata WoO51

Ludwig van Beethoven
(1770–1827)

From the Schott edition *Classical Piano Anthology 3* (ED 13440)

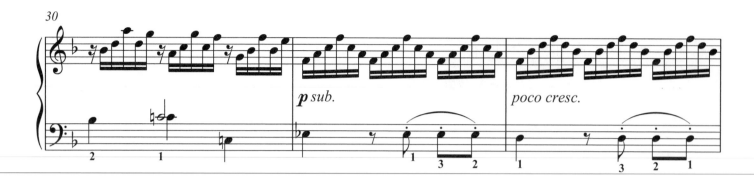

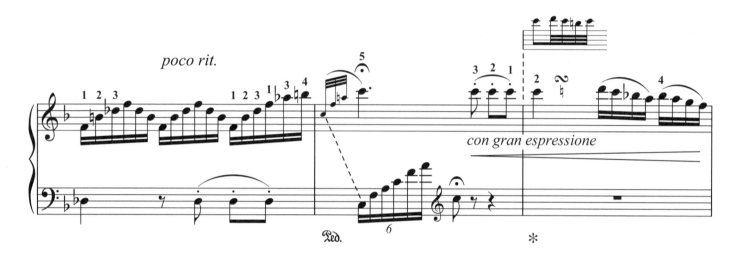

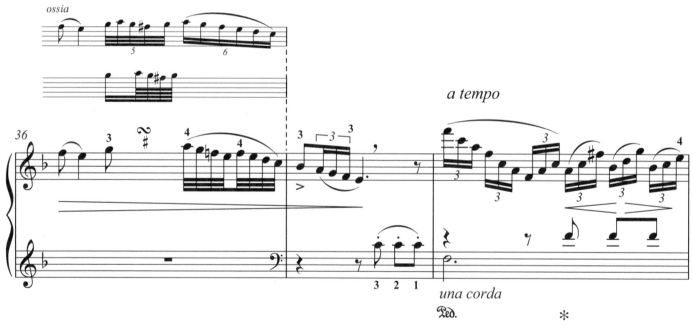

This page is left blank to save an unnecessary page turn.

Moonlight Sonata

from Piano Sonata in C sharp minor, 1st movement

Op. 27/2

Ludwig van Beethoven
(1770–1827)

From the Schott edition *Pianissimo: Liebestraum* (ED 20573)

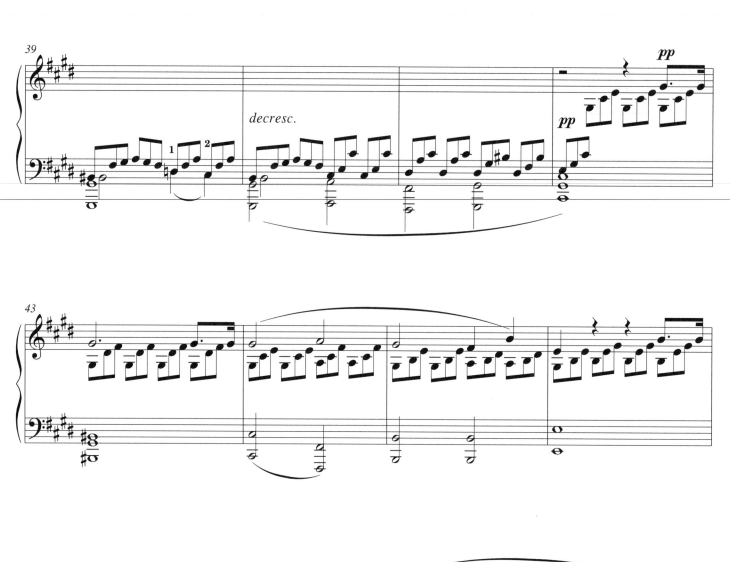

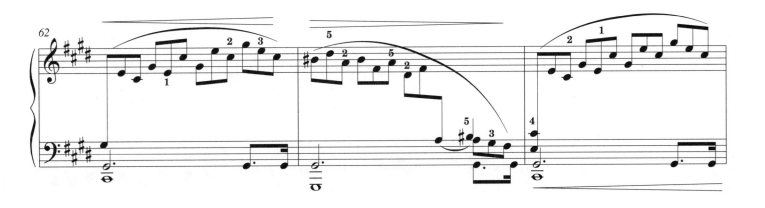

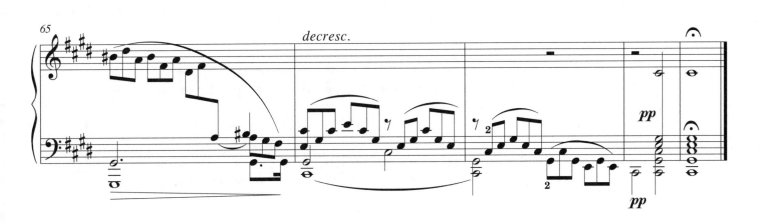

Impromptu

A♭ major

D 935/2

Franz Schubert
(1797–1828)

From the Schott edition *Best of Piano Classics* (ED 9060)

Adagio
Hob. XV: 22/2

Joseph Haydn
(1732–1809)

Adagio ma non troppo
(♩ = 72)

From the Schott edition *Classical Piano Anthology 3* (ED 13440)

This page is left blank to save an unnecessary page turn.

Pathétique
from Piano Sonata in C minor, 2nd movement
Op. 13

Ludwig van Beethoven
(1770–1827)

Adagio cantabile

From the Schott edition *Pianissimo: Liebestraum* (ED 20573)

Adagio
D178

Franz Schubert
(1797–1828)

From the Schott edition *Classical Piano Anthology 4* (ED 13443)

Andante Cantabile
from Sonata No. 8

Wolfgang Amadeus Mozart
(1756–1791)

Andante cantabile con espressione

*) Contrasts between *p* and *f* should not bee too violent. / Ne pas marquer brusquement les contrastes entre piano et forte. /
Gegensätze zwischen *p* und *f* ohne Schroffheit!

From the Schott edition *Sonata in A minor* (ED0 632)

Moment Musical
Op. 94/6

Franz Schubert
(1797–1828)

From the Schott edition *Schubert: Selected Works* (ED 510)

Trio

Allegretto Da Capo senza repetizione al Fine

Adagio
KV 540

Wolfgang Amadeus Mozart
(1756–1791)

From the Schott edition *Classical Piano Anthology 4* (ED 13443)

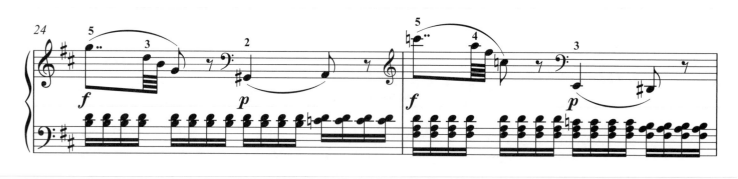

This page is left blank to save an unnecessary page turn.

Impromptu
Op. 90/3

Franz Schubert
(1797–1828)
composed 1827 (G flat Major 𝄵)
appeared 1855 (G Major 𝄵)

*) 𝄵 = Four minim measure. The minims are to be taken "andante", and are therefore not to be dragged. /
  𝄵 = mesure à 4 blanches. Leur jeu est "à enchainer" sans trainer. /
  𝄵 = Vierhalbe-Takt. Die Halben sind andante ("gehend") zu nehmen. Also nicht schleppen!

From the Schott edition *Impromptu* (ED0 654)

Schott Music Ltd, London S&Co.9285